GIGGLE-LOT

JOKES FOR KIDS

BACK TO SCHOOL EDITION

L.E. FUNT

Ideas for using this Joke Book for Kids

PRACTICE TELLING JOKES TO MAKE PEOPLE LAUGH

Memorize one or two of your favorite jokes in this book. Practice them by yourself. When you're ready, find someone to tell the jokes to and make them laugh!

JOKE TELLING CHALLENGE

You and a friend take turns telling jokes to each other while trying not to laugh. When one of you laughs at a joke the one telling it earns a point. Whoever gets three points first is the winner!

OR...ENJOY READING THE JOKES YOURSELF

And have your own secret GiggleFest!

Why should you never argue with a ninety degree angle?

Because it's always right!

Why did Jimmy bring a skunk to show-and-tell?

He thought it was show-and-smell!

Why did the elephant have to stay home from school?

Because he was ill-ephant!

Where did the grammar teacher store all her birthday gifts?

In the present tents!

Why did the professor's dog come to school with him every day?

Because he was teacher's pet

Which foreign language did the plumbers son study?

F-wrench

Which animal is no fun to hang out with at recess?
A playgroundhog

Knock knock
Who's there?
Thea
Thea who?
Theatre nerds are so dramatic!

What do actors in the school play wear to bed?
Drama pajamas!

Why did the girl throw paint on her test?

So she could pass with flying colors!

Brain Teaser:

Why is it called playing piano when it's so much work to learn?

Why did the girl make so much noise when she went down the hall?

She was wearing bell bottoms!

Knock knock
Who's there?
Vanessa
Vanessa who?
Vanessa next history test?

Knock knock
Who's there?
Wilma
Wilma who?
Wilma school uniform be ironed soon?

Julia has 8 slices of pizza. She eats 5. What does she have now?

A stomach ache

What kind of board does the teacher prefer - a chalkboard or whiteboard?

A skateboard!

Which school serves ice cream with chocolate sauce?

Sundae school

Why did the boy take rock climbing equipment to school?
Because he wanted to go to high school

Why did the cookie stay home from school?
It was feeling crumby

Knock knock
Who's there?
Artie
Artie who?
Artie kids ready? It's time for lunch!

What did the teacher get for Valentine's Day?

A heart-shaped box of chalk

What are the sparkliest books?

Classic glitterature

Who teaches pre-school chickens?

Teachirps

What does a teachirp use to write lessons on?
A chick-board

What was the wizard's favorite school subject?
Spell-ing

What is the taxi driver's favorite school subject?
Vo-cab-ulary

What did the doe ask everyone to sign at the end of the school year?
Her deer-book

Why did the drama teacher have to send her student to the vice-principal's office?
He was acting up again!

How did five tables suddenly appear when a minute ago there was only one?
They were multiplication tables

What's the teacher's favorite candy?
Smarties!

Tongue Twister:
Star students shouldn't choose sloppy cheat sheets

Why did the photography teacher have to scrub down her classroom?
It was full of shutterbugs

What kind of band likes to stretch musically?

A rubber band

Why did the baked beans go to the school picnic?

Because they were feeling pot-lucky

Why was the chicken sent to the principal's office?

For using fowl language!

Why did the cow go to school?
To learn moo-sic

Tongue Twister:
Cheeky schoolboys shouldn't chase speedy Spanish students

Knock knock
Who's there?
Orange
Orange who?
Orange you glad that school starts tomorrow?

Why did the girl do dishes while she studied?

So the information would sink in

Knock knock

Who's there?

Eraser

Eraser who?

Eraser to the playground and he beat her!

Tongue Twister

Miss Day gave praise and lots of A's

Who won the school art contest?

It was a draw

Which school subject sounds like soda pop?

Fizz-ics (physics)

Which band did Penny Pig play in?

The school pork-estra!

Brain Teaser:
Why is called HIStory and not OURstory?

Knock knock
Who's there?
Me
Me who?
Meet me on the ballfield after school!

Why did the student have to wash his hands after language class?
He was taking Germ-an

How far do you have to ride your bike to school?

All the way

Why did the eaglet decorate her claws?

She was entering the school talon show

In which month do loggers' kids start the school year?

SepTIMBERRRRR!

Why did Alice text her quiz answers to the teacher?

She wanted textra-credit

Why does the chimpanzee like recess?

He loves the monkey bars

When do they serve candy and soda in the cafeteria?

On the 12th of never!

Why is the classroom so lit up?
It has the brightest students

Which room at the school makes people sad?
The cafe-tear-ia

Why did the bus driver drive fast on the field trip?
They were going to Mt. RUSHmore

What did the 3rd-grader say when her food tray fell?

"Lunch is on me!"

Why did the school band bring PB&J sandwiches to band practice?

They were having a jam session

Knock knock

Who's there?

Lettuce

Lettuce who?

Lettuce out of school early today!

What vitamin is found in honey?

Vitamin bee!

Why did the spider keep an eye in all directions?

He was doing a web search

What did the wasp use to clean the chalkboard?

A bee-raser

Knock knock
Who's there?
Mari
Mari who?
Marine Biology is my best subject!

What kind of sign helps you add numbers?
A plus sign

What kind of test is most refreshing on a hot day?
A pop quiz

Tongue twister:
Forty poor pelican pupils planted fifty-four pink plastic flamingoes

What's the best time of day to study pines, oaks, and maples?
Tree o'clock

What kind of dog loves science class?
A lab

27

Knock knock
Who's there?
Ev
Ev who?
Everyone in the pool, time for swim lessons!

Why do they use trays in the cafeteria?
To avoid flying saucers!

Why did the mischievous boy take a cooking class?
He wanted to stir things up!

Knock knock
Who's there?
Al
Al who?
Al meet you by your locker after class!

When is it okay to call your teacher?
When you're stuck inside your locker!

Why did the teacher make her class write with dull pencils?
She didn't get the point

Why did the school cook hit the lunches with a bat?

She was making club sandwiches

Knock knock

Who's there?

Avery

Avery who?

Avery-body line up for a fire drill!

Why did the boy turn in a wet term paper?

He used a fountain pen!

What kind of doctor did the ruler go to?

A foot doctor!

Knock knock

Who's there?

Imus

Imus who?

I must have forgotten to do my homework!

Tongue twister

Heather's heavy sweater was hot in cold weather

What did one glue stick say to the other?

Let's stick together

Which school administrator comes from royalty?

The prince-ipal

Where does a pilot check out books?

The sky-brary

Why was the private detective snooping around the library?
He needed to check out his client's story

How do trees get on the internet?
They log in

What is a python's favorite school subject?
Hiss-tory

Tongue Twister:
Two foolish students slowly stewed forty purple prunes

How did pioneer acting teachers make their way out West?
By stage-coach

What do bus drivers do after dropping off students?
They take a long brake

Why did the apple suddenly start moving sideways off the teacher's desk?

It was a crab-apple!

Why did the school play audience seem a little unusual?

Because they were in the odd-itorium!

Why did the wasp stand off to the side during the fire drill?

She was making a bee line

What did the crayon say to the colored pencil?

You're looking sharp!

Where does a pen go after breaking the law?

The penitentiary

What happens when a pen gets sick?

They give it penicillin

What do you call a cat who steals another cat's test?

A cheetah

Why did the inventor write a book?

He had a novel idea!

Why did the first-grader get suspended for gambling?

She made an alpha-bet!

How did the pen salesman get through the Panama Canal?

On a pen-man-ship

Why did the girl save pens after they were empty?

She wanted to write with invisible ink

Who uses pom-poms to get you to make your bed?

Choreleaders

When is a running coach also a conductor?

When he trains at the track

Knock knock

Who's there?

Artie

Artie who?

Artiem is red hot! Your team ain't doodly-squat!

What did the pen do with its game show winnings?

Moved into a penthouse

What are dogs with pom-poms called?

A pup squad

Tongue twister:

Lazy lunch ladies ladle slowly

What food did the opera student eat to warm up her voice?

Hum-mus

What do a circus and a school binder have in common?

They both have three rings

What breed of dog makes the best lunch lady?

Chow chow

What happened when the football coach paid a dollar for a 75¢ hot dog?

He got a quarterback!

Knock knock
Who's there?
Jim
Jim who?
J'impress your teachers today?!

What did the alarm clock do when it was still hungry?
Went back four seconds

Where is it OK to tell a little fib?
The school lie-brary

Knock knock
Who's there?
Terri
Terri who?
Terrible news about your D in math

Where do smart picnic pests go to shake their legs?
The school d-ants

What kind of cat works in the school printing office?
A copy cat!

Knock knock
Who's there?
Justin
Justin who?
Just in time for soccer practice!

Why did the girl bring a shoe horn in her lunch bag?
She was trying to fit in at her new school

What do you do if your dog chews up your homework?
Take the words out of his mouth!

Knock knock
Who's there?
Handsome
Handsome who?
Hand some fries to me, I'm hungry!

Knock knock
Who's there?
Ari
Ari who?
Ari ready to walk to school?

Tongue Twister:
Smart schoolkids wear thick-soled shoes

Knock knock
Who's there?
Ron
Ron who?
Ron a little faster so we don't miss the bus!

What did the kitty order for lunch in the cafeteria?
Cold cats on rye with meowstard

Where the best place for twins to study French?
Pair-is

Why couldn't Jacob wear his sneakers on the basketball court?

Because they were tennis shoes

Knock knock

Who's there?

Panda

Panda who?

Pandamonium! Food fight in the school lunchroom!

What do you call a really long phone message?

A text book

Knock knock

Who's there?

Jan

Jan who?

Janitor Bob helped me clean out my locker

Who do circus school students talk to about their problems?

The school clown-selor!

Why did the school bus driver keep driving in circles?

He was a little loopy

Knock knock
Who's there?
Pooch
Pooch who?
Pooch your backpack on so we can go to the library

What happens when you jump too hard on the school trampoline?
Spring Break!

Why did the boy bring a magnifying glass to school?
He made a big deal out of everything

Why did the mouse become a teacher?
She loved squeaking to her students

What did the new bee at school say when he saw his friends?
"What's the buzz?"

Knock knock
Who's there?
Yukon
Yukon who?
Yukon come over after school

Knock knock
Who's there?
Taylor
Taylor who?
Taylor that I'll come as soon as class is out

Tongue twister:
Penny prized pastel paint for polka-dotted paper flowers

Why did the girl wear a rain hat to school?
She was under the weather

How did the rodent get on the football team?

He was enor-mouse!

Why did the girl take belly-dancing classes?

She dreamed of joining the Naval Academy

Knock knock

Who's there?

Otto

Otto who?

Auto shop is cancelled today, the mechanic is on a road trip!

Knock knock
Who's there?
Bill
Bill who?
Bill-ieve me, I'm ready for school to start!

Why did the boy get in trouble for something he didn't do?
He didn't do his homework!

Why do some kids hate math?
They don't like all the problems

How did the young seamstress do on her tailoring test?

Sew-sew

Why couldn't the halftime band play in January?

Because it was a March-ing band

Why did the runner eat beef jerky at the competition?

He was at a track meat

Knock knock
Who's there?
Sara
Sara who?
Sara pop quiz on Friday?

Why is the school bus lady so lousy at putting?
Because she's a driver

Where do little cowpokes learn to use a lasso?
In the classo-room!

What does PE stand for?

Play energetically

What does PE stand for after class?

Physical exhaustion

Knock knock

Who's there?

Sherwood

Sherwood who?

Sherwood like pizza for lunch

Knock knock
Who's there?
Elsie
Elsie who?
Elsie if my mom will drive us to the soccer game

What did the paper say to the eraser?
You rub me the wrong way!

What advice did the bug have for new students?
Bee yourself

How do you spell Panda with 2 letters?

P and A

Why don't they serve sushi fishsticks at school?

It's a half-baked idea!

Knock knock

Who's there?

Alaska

Alaska who?

Alaska librarian which state is the coldest

Where does the little vampire get his grades at year's end?

On his creeport card

Knock knock

Who's there?

Flute

Flute who?

Flew to Florida for Spring Break!

Who won the giraffe races at the track meet?

It was neck and neck

59

Why was the whale so happy with his test grade?

Because it was a-sea (a C)

How did the spider gather information for her report on flies?

She searched the web

Why was the 8-legged sea creature able to leave class?

He had an octo-pass

Which room has the best view and most comfortable chairs, but you don't want to go there?
The principal's office

What do you call a group of school tents set up in the woods?
A camp-us

Where does a young cow eat his school lunch?
In the calf-eteria

61

Tongue Twister:
Silly Polly spilled her little pickle bottle

Why don't they teach about dogs at school?
So cats won't get jealous!

Tongue Twister
Iris eyed an Irish wristwatch

Why do they teach percentages in math class?
They're 80% sure you need to know them

Where was the Declaration of Independence signed?
On the bottom

Why don't some American kids know about the English Channel?
Because they can't get it on TV

Where can you go to learn about bridges?

Connect-icut

Which state has the most crayons?

Color-ado

Knock knock

Who's there?

Iowa

Iowa who?

Iowa lot to my teachers

In which state does everyone wear clean clothes?

Washing-ton

Which state has the most hospitals?

Ill-inois

How did Bonnie guess what they were serving in the cafeteria?

She had a lunch hunch

Why weren't the football players scared of the locker room ghost?

Because it had team spirit

Where are schoolchildren most likely to wander out of their classroom?

Rome

How did Santa's helper practice his penmanship?

By writing the elf-abet

Where do pillow children learn to read and write?

They are usually foam-schooled

What should you wear to school on test day?

Smarty-pants!

Knock knock

Who's there?

Ella

Ella who?

Ellaphant's on the loose in the hallway!

Why did the student bring her diary to class?

Because she goes to private school

Why were the kids in computer lab shivering?

Because it was code in there!

Where do men in armor attend class?

Knight School

Tongue Twister
Bree banged her headboard and ripped her blue bedspread

Why did the cat make up a story about forgetting his homework?
Because he was a-lyin' (a lion)

How do you decide what to do when it's rainy?
Have a brainstorm!

What do you call it when a book report is due and there's a math test on the same day?

Being over-booked

Why did the pen join Facebook?

It was looking for a pen pal!

Why did the mother goat buy a mini van?

To bring her kids to school

Knock knock
Who's there?
Willie
Willie who?
Willie tell me the answers to the test?

Brain Teaser
If you do homework in the car is it called carwork?

Who flies home when class is out?
A bee student

Tongue Twister

Few students viewed the huge kangaroo

What is Miss Puss's favorite school class?

Mew-sic

Where did the young students learn how to plant vegetables?

In kinder-garden

Where do little cabooses go to learn?

The train-ing center

Knock knock

Who's there?

Wendy

Wendy who?

Wendy school bell rings we can go out and play!

How did the Bighorn sheep prepare for his test?

He c-RAMmed for it

Where does a golf pro learn how to hit off the tee?

Driving school

What grades will you find on a hornet's report card?

Straight bees

Which class is Little Kitty's favorite?

FURst PURRiod

Why did the chicken cross the playground?
To get to the other slide!

What do they serve for lunch at beaver school?
Damburgers

Knock knock
Who's there?
Dewey
Dewey who?
Dewey have any sandwiches?
It's lunchtime!

Why did the sparkler get A's on all his tests?

He was brilliant

Tongue Twister

Is that your teacher in the bleachers or another tougher instructor?

Knock knock

Who's there?

Luke

Luke who?

Luke out! There's a ball coming at your head!

Knock knock
Who's there?
Hugo
Hugo who?
Hugo right at the corner to get to the gym

Why did the school nurse use a red pen?
In case she needed to draw blood

Tongue Twister
You borrowed my backpack a while back. Can I have my pack back?

Why did the boy get bus money and saltines for a science fair prize?

He won fare and square!

Tongue Twister

Preschool in Liverpool has a wading pool with a step stool

Knock knock

Who's there?

Dawn

Dawn who?

Dawn forget there's a dance after school. Everyone's going!

Why couldn't the troll come out to play after school?

He had to finish his gnomework

How did the Ketchikan girl like her classes?

I don't know, Alaska!

Knock knock

Who's there?

Fess

Fess who?

Fess up! You love school!

Eight American students and two teachers were studying in a boat. Where were they?

Ten-asea

Where do Florida pigs go to college?

Mi-hammy State

Where is the best city to study dentistry?

Floss Angeles

Which continent is always on deck in baseball?

Europe (you're up)

What school snacks are on the metric system?

Gram crackers

How often does the hairdressing student attend class?

Only part-time

If a dog can learn to sit, stay, and fetch, why can't he learn the A-B-C's?
Because it's im-paw-sible!

Tongue Twister:
Clocks tick, clocks tock, kids crowd the crosswalks

Where do chimpanzees go for basketball practice?
The jungle gym

Knock knock
Who's there?
Arthur
Arthur who?
Arthur any clubs after school we can join?

Knock knock
Who's there?
Ivan
Ivan who?
Ivan an idea. Let's join the golf club!

What do you call a quiz you didn't study for?

A guessing game!

Tongue Twister

A teacher and a creature went to a double feature

Knock knock

Who's there?

Hope

Hope who?

Hope we don't have to run laps in PE again

Knock knock
Who's there?
Howl
Howl who?
Howl I get into the choir if I can't sing?

Knock knock
Who's there?
Mabel
Mabel who?
Mabel if you practice you can do better!

85

What's the best present to give your choir teacher?
Earplugs!

Knock knock
Who's there?
Oliver
Oliver who?
Oliver sudden the teacher started laughing

If you write a story with a happy ending, is that bad?
Only if everyone's happy it ended!

What kind of classwork is quite refreshing?

Assign-mints

Knock knock

Who's there?

Livia

Livia who?

Livia best school life!

Which students are quiet even as they are talking?

Sign language students

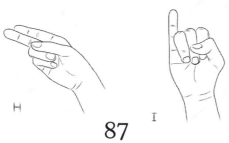

Why did Sammy bring a full glass of water to English class?
He heard there was going to be a spilling test

What kind of dog might you find in the school cafeteria?
A lunch box-er

What common greeting is hidden in consecutive alphabet letters?
Hi!!

What gymnastics move was popular among pioneer children?

Ox-cartwheels

What do flea children say at the beginning of each school day?

The Pledge of A-flea-gence

Where do astronaut's kids eat their midday meals?

The school launchroom

Where do little seagulls change after gym class?

The flocker room

What happened when 19 and 20 got into a fight?

21

What did the Orca say on his first day of school?

Whale you come out for recess?

Brain Teaser

Can an elephant be light on its feet?

Why did the history teacher give homework assignments every day?

Because history repeats itself!

Why did the girl go to a fast food restaurant to research her paper?

Because she was writing about Greece

Knock knock
Who's there?
Maya
Maya who?
My arithmetic homework is overdue!

How can you tell when someone has trouble with penmanship?
They cross their eyes

What do you have to pay to go to school?
Attention!

What motivates kids to learn new things?

Tests!

Why did X, V and I wander around the school?

Because they were Roman numerals!

Why are cats good at organizing their homework?

They put things into CATegories!

How do you pass an i test?
Remember to put a dot on it

Tongue Twister
Flint flung French fries far afield

How does a kitten show her parents her grades?
On her re-purrt card

Tongue Twister:
Charlie showed six chipped
chalkboards to Sharon

Knock knock
Who's there?
Archie
Archie who?
**Are cheese sandwiches on the
school lunch menu today?**

Brain Teaser:
If there are pop quizzes, why aren't
there mom quizzes?

Tongue Twister:
The student's poodle somehow straddled the puddle

How do gnomes get to school?
They ride in a mini-bus

Why was the kangaroo studying geneology?
She wanted to find her kangaroots

Why did the Australian bear go to university?
To get a koala-ty education

What country conducts the most pop quizzes?
CANada

Brain Teaser:
If there are crayons, why aren't there crayoffs?

Where did the goat kids gather for the pep rally?

At the assembleat!

What kind of drill did the school janitor use to get out of work?

A fire drill

What happened when the athlete forgot her skates for the big hockey game?

Nothing, it was field hockey

What did the magical horse have to wear to school?
A unicorn uniform

How did the two heads of school know each other?
They were princi-pals

Knock knock
Who's there?
Java
Java who?
Java nice summer vacation?

Tongue Twister:
Should teachers with peaches avoid sandy beaches?

Where did the teacher keep her pens near the window?
On the pen-sills

Brain Teaser:
If you write with your left hand, how do you wrong?

Why did the teacher have to move to the chalkboard in the back?

Because the one in front was chalk-full

What did the librarian do when she heard there was a kidnapping?

She woke him up!

How do cattle do their math homework?

With a cowculator!

Why did the students eat their homework?

Their teacher told them it was a piece of cake!

Which school subject are fleas really good at?

Arithme-tick

Why did the cell phone get a Nobel prize?

It was a smart phone

Why were the school uniforms red, blue and yellow?

It was a primary school!

Why did the clock get sent to the principal's office?

For tocking too much!

Knock knock

Who's there?

Mel

Mel who?

Mel locker is too full

Why did the girl put a flashlight in her lunch bag?

She wanted a light lunch

Knock knock

Who's there?

Ya

Ya who?

Yahoo! It's my last class for the week!

Why was the student's report card wet?

Because it was below C level

How can you make seven even?

Take away the "S"

Where does an elephant sit in home room?

Wherever he wants!

Knock knock

Who's there?

Anita

Anita who?

Anita pencil. Can I borrow one?

Knock knock
Who's there?
Ahmed
Ahmed who?
Ahmed a mistake, can I borrow an eraser?

Knock knock
Who's there?
Ivan
Ivan who?
Ivan another piece of paper. I made too many mistakes!

Why was the broom late for school?
It overswept!

Look for these **GIGGLE**FEST books on Amazon:

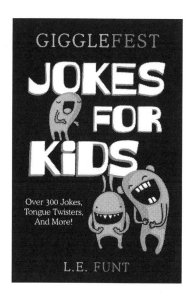

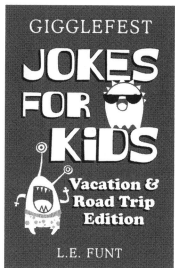

Follow us on Facebook:

www.facebook.com/gigglefestforkids

Made in the USA
Middletown, DE
09 September 2019